Date: 9/19/12

J 359.96 LOR
Loria, Laura.
Marine Force Recon /

US SPECIAL FORCES

MARINE FORCE RECON

By Laura Loria

Gareth Stevens
Publishing

Please visit our website, www.garethstevens.com. For a free color catalog of all our high-quality books, call toll free 1-800-542-2595 or fax 1-877-542-2596.

Library of Congress Cataloging-in-Publication Data

Loria, Laura.
Marine Force Recon / Laura Loria.
    p. cm. — (US special forces)
Includes index.
ISBN 978-1-4339-6563-0 (pbk.)
ISBN 978-1-4339-6564-7 (6-pack)
ISBN 978-1-4339-6561-6 (library binding)
1. United States. Marine Corps. Force Reconnaissance—Juvenile literature. 2. United States. Marine Corps—Commando troops—Juvenile literature. I. Title.
VE23.L66 2012
359.9'6—dc23

                                        2011029446

First Edition

Published in 2012 by
Gareth Stevens Publishing
111 East 14th Street, Suite 349
New York, NY 10003

Copyright © 2012 Gareth Stevens Publishing

Designer: Michael J. Flynn
Editor: Kristen Rajczak

Photo credits: Cover, p. 1 MILpictures by Tom Weber/The Image Bank/Getty Images; photos courtesy of US Marines: pp. 4–5 by Sgt. Jeremy Ross, 6, 9, 15 by Lance Clp. Reece E. Lodder, 7 by Gunnery Sgt. Mark Oliva, 11 by Cpl. Nicole A. LaVine, 12 by Cpl. Claudio A. Martinez, 13 by Lance Cpl. Casey Jones, 14 by Pfc. John Robbart III, 16–17 by SSgt. Danielle Bacon, 24 by E-5/MC2 Marcos T. Hernandez, 25 by Lance Cpl. Jennifer Pirante, 26–27 by B Company, 2nd Reconnaissance, 28–29 by Cmdr. Christopher Nodine; p. 19 Archive Photos/Hulton Archive/Getty Images; pp. 20–21 AFP/Getty Images; pp. 22–23 Robert Sullivan/AFP/Getty Images.

Printed in the United States of America

CPSIA compliance information: Batch #CW12GS: For further information contact Gareth Stevens, New York, New York at 1-800-542-2595.

CONTENTS

Words in the glossary appear in **bold** type the first time they are used in the text.

WHAT IS FORCE RECON?

Imagine you're planning a trip to an unfamiliar place, where you don't know anyone. What would you do before you left? You might read a book, look at a map, or talk to someone who's been there before.

Force Recon marines secretly observe enemy troops.

A Force Recon marine is a guide for military forces. "Recon" is short for "**reconnaissance**." These specially trained marines travel all over the world to collect information the military couldn't otherwise learn. They find safe places for troops to land and help plan **missions**. Sometimes, Marine Force Recon carries out its own missions as well, but its main role is to support larger **units**.

Recon Men

All active Force Recon marines are men. Women can't be appointed to combat, or battle, positions in the US military at this time. Some people think this is unfair. However, women can have supporting roles in the recon reserves, or soldiers who aren't on active duty.

SPECIAL OPS

Force Recon is a special ops, or operations, unit. Force Recon marines work on covert, or secret, missions and are often needed where larger forces won't work. They're trained to operate in the air, on land, or at sea. These men must be patient, sometimes letting enemies get away, in order to observe them and gather **intelligence**.

Force Recon marines work differently from members of the regular Marine Corps. A marine follows orders and carries out a plan mapped out by his commander. A Force Recon marine is ready for many situations and often has to take action on his own.

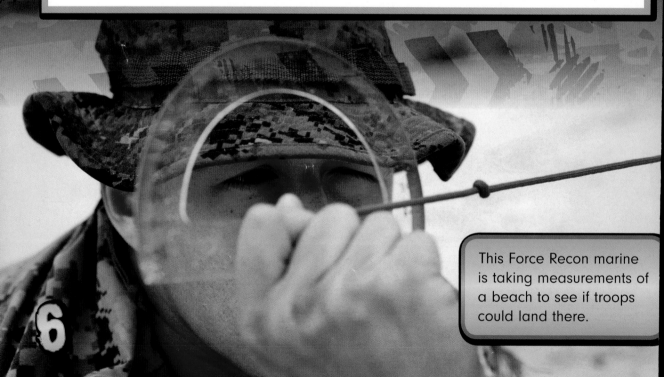

This Force Recon marine is taking measurements of a beach to see if troops could land there.

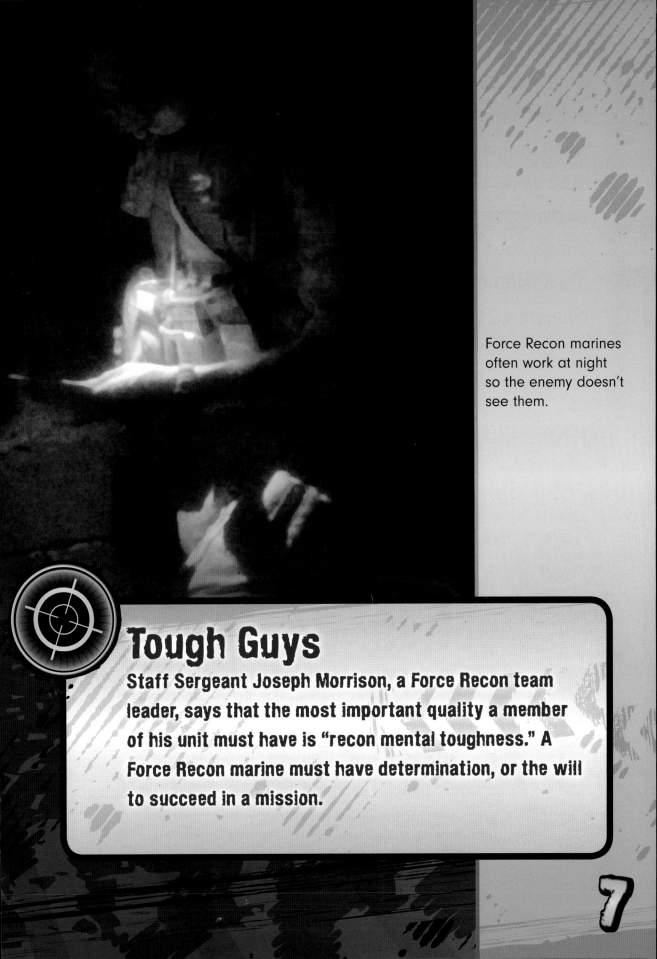

Force Recon marines often work at night so the enemy doesn't see them.

Tough Guys

Staff Sergeant Joseph Morrison, a Force Recon team leader, says that the most important quality a member of his unit must have is "recon mental toughness." A Force Recon marine must have determination, or the will to succeed in a mission.

7

Force Recon marines commonly work in teams of six men, ...ugh more or fewer men may go on certain missions. These ...all teams allow them to move quickly and quietly through an ...a while still carrying enough weapons and supplies. Many ...es, Force Recon teams gather information deep behind ...my lines. Their missions can be very risky!

Some people believe there are three Force Recon ...npanies, each stationed at a different location. However, ...orce Recon operates in secret, there isn't a way to confirm ...v many active companies there are today.

Marine Special Operations School

A US marine who wants to become part of Force Recon has to go to Marine Special Operations School. The Marine Special Operations Individual Course is 7 months long and includes training for battle in small spaces, special reconnaissance, weapons, irregular warfare, and many other areas.

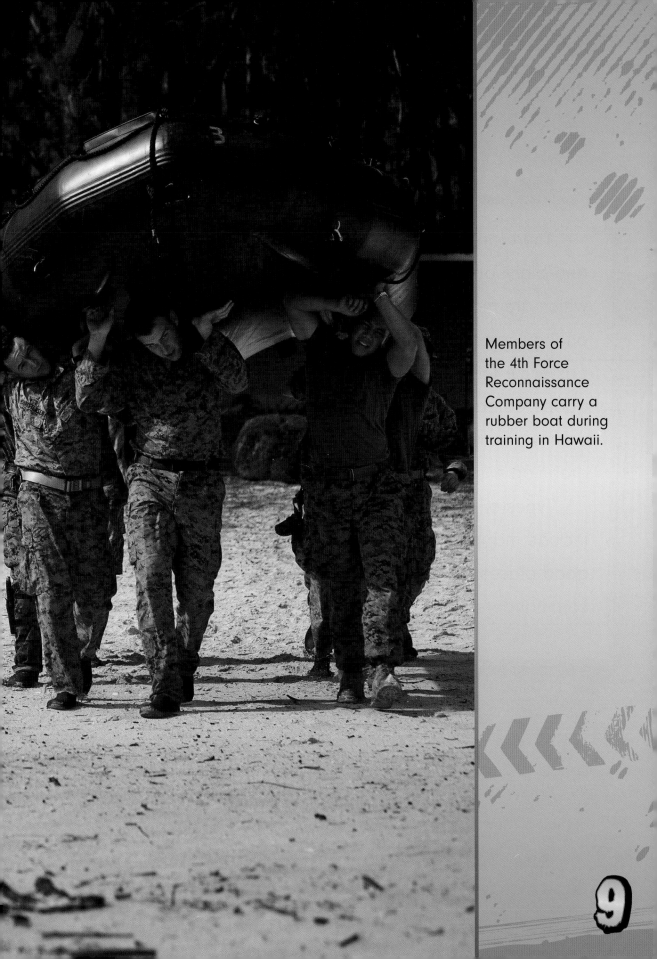

Members of the 4th Force Reconnaissance Company carry a rubber boat during training in Hawaii.

GREEN OPS AND BLACK OPS

There are two types of Force Recon operations: green ops and black ops. Green ops are deep-reconnaissance missions, which are mainly for gathering information. These missions rely on the secrecy of small teams deep behind enemy lines. Green ops occur too deep for the team to be helped by support troops, so each member has to be ready for anything. If the enemy discovers the marines or there are shots fired during a green-op mission, it has failed.

Types of information gathered during a green op may include mapping out roads and waterways, and finding good places to land aircraft. Force Recon marines then notify commanders of these locations.

Keep Your Cool!

Force Recon marines have to be ready to work in all kinds of conditions. For cold weather training, one group of marines went to Alaska to learn how to stay warm while working in snow-covered areas. Their final test was a 23-mile (37 km) mission in below-freezing temperatures.

Force Recon marines may operate on beaches, in the mountains, or in the desert.

Black ops are even more secretive. They involve direct action against an enemy. The goal of a black-op mission is to attack and pull out quickly. During these missions, Force Recon marines may seize ships, oil platforms, or enemy supplies. Black ops may also involve rescuing prisoners, but Force Recon marines aren't commonly part of those missions.

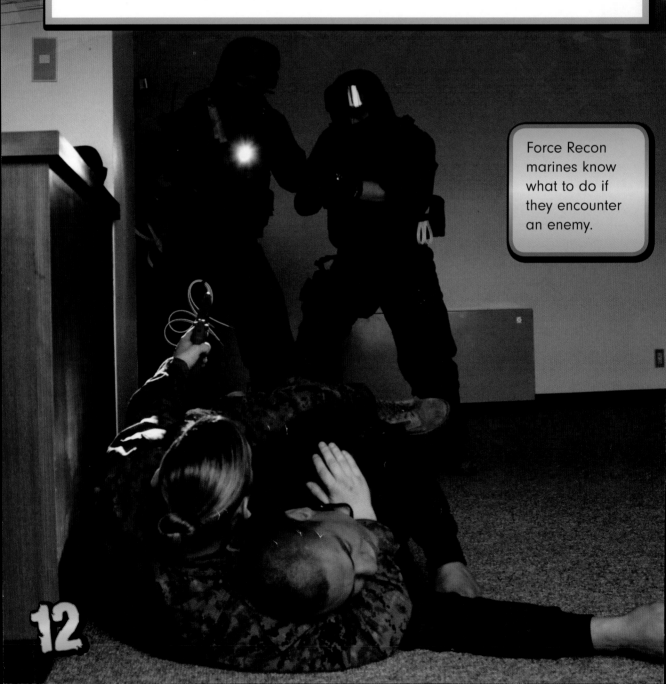

Force Recon marines know what to do if they encounter an enemy.

After completing a mission, members of a black-ops team ~~mu~~st have a plan for quick escape by air, land, or sea. Other ~~team~~s stand by to offer support during these missions and help ~~with~~ quick exits.

Swift. Silent. Deadly.

The official saying of the US Marine Corps is *Semper Fidelis*, which is a Latin phrase that means "Always Faithful." The saying of Force Recon is "Swift. Silent. Deadly." This highlights the main goal of a Force Recon marine: complete a mission quickly and effectively, without anyone knowing.

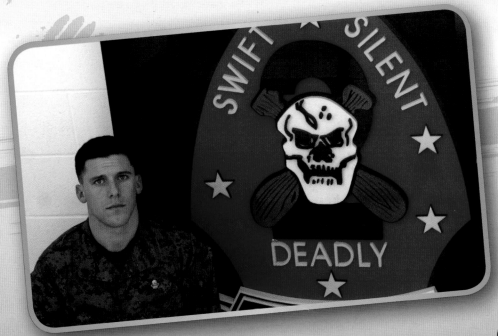

TRAINING

Being physically fit is required for Force Recon marines, who must work in challenging conditions. First, they must train to become part of the US Marine Corps. A marine must be able to run 3 miles (4.8 km) in no more than 28 minutes and do many crunches in 2 minutes.

Force Recon marines must be even faster and stronger than regular marines. Many men who apply for Force Recon training aren't accepted. In order to qualify for training, a marine has to pass a mentally and physically demanding test. It includes sit-ups, push-ups, swimming, and a long hike carrying a heavy pack.

Marines must pass a test to prove their physical fitness every 6 months.

Quiet Strength

Force Recon marines don't spend their workout time trying to build big muscles. It's more important for them to be able to move their bodies easily so they can travel quickly and silently. Some missions may require marines to crouch for a long time, which can be tiring.

A Force Recon marine slides down a rope while training for helicopter operations.

A marine who wants to join Force Recon must have an excellent military record. He also has to be a superior shooter and very smart.

Those who are accepted into training learn many tasks other soldiers don't. Courses such as combat diving, mountain warfare, and airborne training prepare these marines for the different situations they might encounter. They also receive training, such as communications and photography, that focuses on intelligence-gathering skills. Some of the most important training involves learning to move silently and without being seen. These special marines must be prepared to confront an enemy, so they learn skills such as **sniping** as well.

A Force Recon marine prepares to shoot his M4 Carbine.

Force Recon Medical Team

Medical soldiers don't commonly see battle. However, those assigned to Marine Force Recon are trained to fight as well as treat those who are injured. In fact, they're taught to shoot first and care for a patient second.

THE BEGINNINGS OF FORCE RECON

The Marine Force Recon story began during World War II. In 1942, an intelligence-gathering and observation group became part of the 1st Marine Division. It became the **Amphibious** Reconnaissance Company (ARC) the next year. The unit, called the Amphibious Reconnaissance **Battalion** by 1944, worked with the navy on more than 150 reconnaissance missions in the Pacific. They scouted landing locations on Tinian Island, Iwo Jima, and Okinawa.

For the rest of the war, the battalion continued to assist and train with the navy. They learned underwater operations such as **demolition** and diving.

Royal Marine Commandos

Today's Marine Force Recon was formed from the ARC and a group of Raider Battalions. The Raiders were modeled after the British Royal Marine Commandos, who also trained to strike enemies quickly in the air, on land, and at sea.

A marine crouches on a beach during amphibious training in 1945.

FORCE RECON IN KOREA

During the Korean War, the Force Recon marines gathered information about the North Korean enemies. They also helped on **raids** that weakened the enemy supply chain. Working with the navy, they traveled as far as 40 miles (64 km) inland on their missions.

After the Korean War ended, Force Recon training focused on the possibility of **nuclear** war, which meant exploring deeper inland than before. The men learned to parachute from airplanes and land safely in order to gather intelligence.

In 1957, a Parachute Recon Platoon, a Pathfinder Platoon, and an Amphibious Recon Company joined to form the 1st Force Recon Company. Marine Force Recon was now ready for missions at sea, in the air, and on land.

OORAH!

The 1st Company ARC is thought to have coined the marine cry "OORAH" in 1953. It was based on the sound their submarine made before it was about to dive, like an old-fashioned car horn—"ah-ROO-gah!"

US troops land by parachute during the Korean War.

21

FORCE RECON IN VIETNAM

The Vietnam War was different from any war Force Recon marines had fought in before. The enemy was hard to find. US forces weren't ready for this at first. Force Recon marines had to change how they completed missions. Though their first task was reconnaissance, they also lured the enemy out of hiding and fought more often than before.

Force Recon marines have been important parts of conflicts all over the world. These marines are preparing for Operation Desert Shield in 1991.

By the end of the war, Force Recon marines were noted for their bravery in confronting the enemy first, rather than waiting to be discovered. One recon company, code-named Killer Kane, was especially successful at **ambush** operations.

The Gulf War

Force Recon marines played important roles in US operations in the Persian Gulf during the early 1990s. They traveled to Kuwait to watch and report on enemy and border movement. They also scouted routes for US forces to travel, helping soldiers bypass minefields and other obstacles.

GEAR

During the early days of Force Recon, marines had very basic gear. World War II recon marines sometimes carried only knives to defend themselves. While an updated version of that KA-BAR knife is still used by marines, today's Force Recon units have the latest **technology** to aid them in their missions.

Because their job requires them to act like spies, Force Recon marines need high-tech **surveillance** gear. The AN/VPS-14 Monocular Night Vision Device helps them see in the dark and can be held in the hand or mounted onto a helmet. Force Recon marines use global positioning systems (GPS), parachutes, and SCUBA gear, too.

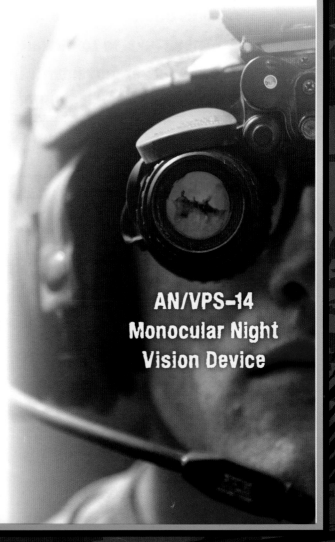

AN/VPS-14 Monocular Night Vision Device

Force Recon marines even have special radio gear to communicate intelligence to other troops.

UTM

When scouting a location, Force Recon marines use the Universal Transverse Mercator (UTM) grid to let commanders know where things are. The UTM grid is a special map grid designed for military use. It was created to avoid some of the problems with earlier map grids and allow locations to be identified more accurately.

FORCE RECON TODAY

After the attacks on the United States that took place on September 11, 2001, the US military's main focus became fighting **terrorism**. Marine Force Recon units are a big part of US efforts to find and break up terrorist groups in Iraq, Afghanistan, and other countries.

These Force Recon marines found many hidden weapons while on duty in Iraq.

Force Recon marines still spend time gathering information to locate enemy hiding places. However, their methods are changing. For Force Recon marines serving in the Middle East, this means being out in the open and showing people they're there to help. They spend more time listening to local citizens than observing in secret.

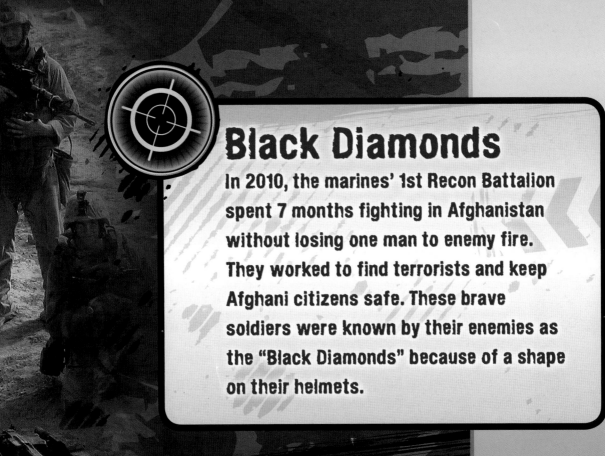

Black Diamonds

In 2010, the marines' 1st Recon Battalion spent 7 months fighting in Afghanistan without losing one man to enemy fire. They worked to find terrorists and keep Afghani citizens safe. These brave soldiers were known by their enemies as the "Black Diamonds" because of a shape on their helmets.

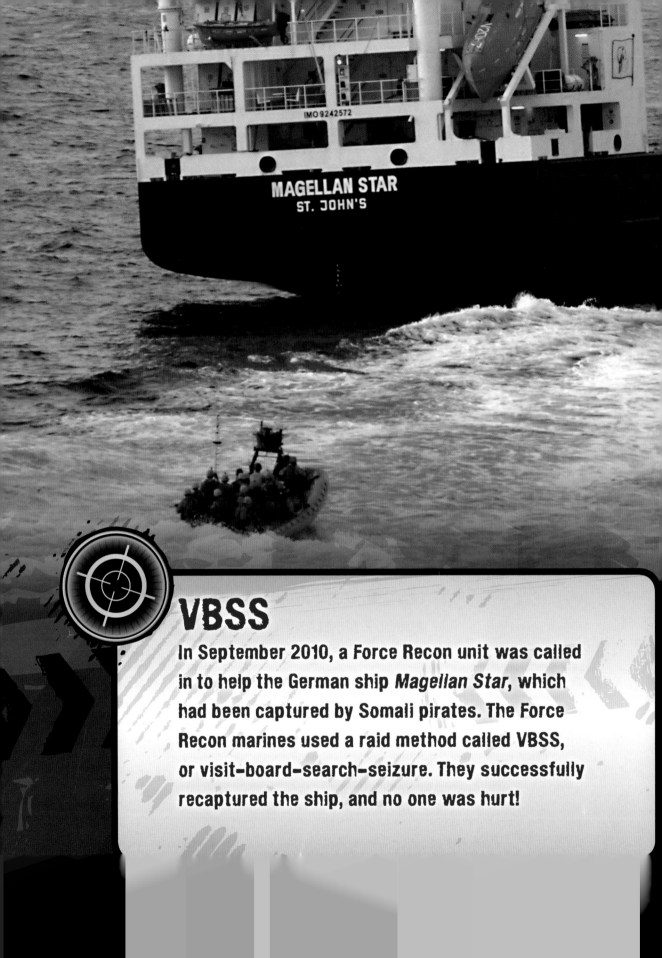

VBSS

In September 2010, a Force Recon unit was called in to help the German ship *Magellan Star*, which had been captured by Somali pirates. The Force Recon marines used a raid method called VBSS, or visit-board-search-seizure. They successfully recaptured the ship, and no one was hurt!

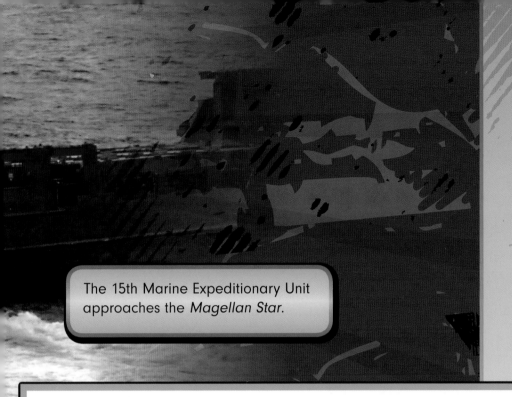

The 15th Marine Expeditionary Unit approaches the *Magellan Star*.

Force Recon marines have always supported other US military forces. In 2006, Force Recon marines became part of the US Marine Corps Special Operations Command (MARSOC), a new grouping within the US Special Operations Command. The reorganization put Force Recon in the company of other specially trained fighting units from all branches of the armed forces.

Today, Force Recon marines continue their covert reconnaissance missions all over the world. The information they gather is valuable. Their bravery and dedication to the protection of Americans and world citizens alike is even more so.

GLOSSARY

ambush: a surprise attack

amphibious: having the capability to operate both on land and in water

battalion: a group in the military made up of two companies and their commanders

demolition: the act of working with explosives to destroy things

intelligence: the gathering of secret information about enemies

mission: a task

nuclear: having to do with the power created by splitting atoms, the smallest bits of an element

raid: a sudden attack

reconnaissance: the exploration of a place to collect information

sniping: shooting well from a hiding place

surveillance: the act of watching someone or something closely

technology: the way people do something using tools and the tools that they use

terrorism: the continuous use of violence and fear to challenge an authority

unit: a group of soldiers that is part of a larger whole

FOR MORE INFORMATION

Books

David, Jack. *Marine Corps Force Recon.* Minneapolis, MN: Bellwether Media, 2009.

Payment, Simone. *Frontline Marines: Fighting in the Marine Combat Arms Unit.* New York, NY: Rosen Central, 2007.

Sandler, Michael. *Marine Force Recon in Action.* New York, NY: Bearport Publishing, 2008.

Websites

Marines
www.marines.com
Learn more about what the marines do.

National Museum of the Marine Corps
www.usmcmuseum.com
Take a virtual tour of the National Museum of the Marine Corps.

U.S. Marine Corps Hymn
kids.niehs.nih.gov/lyrics/marine.htm
Learn the official song of the Marine Corps.

INDEX